HowExpert Presents

Running for Women 101

A Woman's Quick Guide on How to Run Your Fastest Race From the 5K to the Marathon

HowExpert with Jenni Jacobsen

For more tips related to this topic, visit HowExpert.com/runningforwomen.

Recommended Resources

- HowExpert.com – Quick 'How To' Guides on All Topics from A to Z by Everyday Experts.
- HowExpert.com/free – Free HowExpert Email Newsletter.
- HowExpert.com/books – HowExpert Books
- HowExpert.com/courses – HowExpert Courses
- HowExpert.com/membership – HowExpert Membership Site
- HowExpert.com/writers – Write About Your #1 Passion/Knowledge/Expertise & Become a HowExpert Author.
- HowExpert.com/resources – Additional HowExpert Recommended Resources
- YouTube.com/HowExpert – Subscribe to HowExpert YouTube.
- Instagram.com/HowExpert – Follow HowExpert on Instagram.
- Facebook.com/HowExpert – Follow HowExpert on Facebook.

Table of Contents

Chapter 1: Introduction to the Arena of Women's running

Women's Enthusiastic Participation in Running Events

Women are passionate about running. In fact, long distance running is so popular among women that they outnumber men in participation in road racing events. According to Running USA, women comprised 57 percent of road race finishers in 2016, outnumbering men 9.7 million to 7.3 million. This trend has persisted since 2010 when women constituted 53 percent of road race finishers; their participation has consistently outpaced men's, slightly increasing over the past six years and remaining stable at 57 percent since 2013 ("US Road Race Trends"). Women are especially attracted to half marathon races, as they made up 61 percent of half marathon finishers in 2015, per Running USA. Women also dominated 5k and 10k races, comprising 59 percent and 58 percent of participants, respectively ("2016 State of the Sport").

The increase in women's participation in long distance races represents a profound social movement that began centuries ago. Pauline has explained that after Katherine Switzer was the first woman to officially register for and run the Boston Marathon in 1967, at a time when society did not permit women to participate in marathons, there was a cultural movement characterized by women competing in road races and other endurance events (4). One year prior to Switzer's heroic performance, Roberta Gibb was the first woman to run the Boston Marathon as an unregistered participant. Gibb had attempted to register for the race, but the Boston Athletic Association rejected her effort to enter and advised her that women were not permitted to run over 1.5 miles, and that women were incapable of running a race of 26.2 miles, because it was too far of a distance for them. Gibb dismissed this notion and competed in the race without an official bib. (Burfoot 43-44).

Despite Switzer and Gibb making the first female appearances in the Boston Marathon in 1967 and 1966, it wasn't until almost 20 years later, in 1984, when the first women's marathon was introduced to the Olympics. Joan Benoit was the first female to cross the finish line, significantly outrunning the rest of the field (Burfoot introduction).

Benoit's accomplishment was groundbreaking for female athletes, but Burfoot has argued that it wasn't until the 1990s that women began running in droves, after Oprah Winfrey's monumental participation in the 1994 Marine Corps Marathon. Oprah's performance was especially pivotal for the women's running movement, as Oprah grew up in a troubled environment and belonged to a racial group not commonly known for distance running, at least not in the United States. Oprah sent a message to fellow women that if she could run a marathon, they certainly could too (Burfoot introduction).

Oprah has unequivocally had a profound impact on other women, as females have dominated the world of running in recent years. Women enthusiastically participate in charity races, organized races to fight against breast cancer, women-only events, and family races at amusement parks such as Disney World. Look around at the starting line of any local road race, and the field will be full of women of all ages, body types, and ability levels. Some run to stay healthy and fit, while others run for camaraderie and socialization. Still others run to be competitive or to meet personal goals. Whatever their reason for running, it is clear that women have left their mark in the arena of long distance running.

Unique Challenges of Female Runners

Despite the explosion in women's running throughout the past several decades, female runners continue to experience unique challenges. One such difficulty is women's obligation to raise their children, which can deter them from training for and participating in running events. Tsang and Havitz conducted a study with adults who had previously run college level cross-country, and they found that the addition of children to the family was associated with less running, especially among women (45). After childbirth, women often must take time to recover and bond with their new babies, making running impossible during the early postpartum period. Even as babies grow older, the demands of raising a child can leave little time or energy for running, especially for mothers who are still awakened multiple times each night by a crying baby. Pregnancy can also lead to weight gain that renders running more difficult, and some women might find running after childbirth to be painful. Beyond the changes that occur immediately following pregnancy and childbirth, mothers often make sacrifices throughout their children's lives, putting their children's needs first and neglecting their own needs. For instance, women might be so committed to spending time with their children, assisting with homework, managing the household, and working to provide for their families that they lack the time to devote to running.

In addition to challenges associated with motherhood, women demonstrate physiological differences that can make running more challenging for them than for men. Joyner has explained that elite women tend to run 10 to 12 percent slower than men do, which is likely a result of women having a lower VO_2 max (2949). In addition, women tend to have more body fat than men of a comparable weight do, as well as a lower red cell mass when compared to men of an equal weight. Furthermore, women usually have smaller lungs, relative to their body sizes, than men do (Joyner 2952). Cheuvront et al. have also concluded that men tend to outperform women in running, because they possess stronger muscles and larger aerobic capacities (1017).

Beyond the physiological mechanisms that cause women to run more slowly than men, they can also struggle with body image issues that undermine their performance. Cultural and societal ideals may pressure women to stay thin and lean, but female runners can feel especially compelled to maintain a stereotypical slender runner's build. The research has demonstrated the reality of this struggle. Anderson et al. found that female runners displayed higher levels of body dissatisfaction and more eating disorder symptoms than men did. Specifically, women who ran

5k and 10k races scored higher on an Eating Attitudes Test, which can be indicative of an eating disorder (43). Women therefore experience a unique struggle and may be susceptible to disordered eating patterns that can interfere with their health and running performance.

Related to disordered eating is the concern of the female athlete triad among women who run. In a review of this condition, Matzkin et al. explained that the female athlete triad involves one of the following three factors: low energy availability, abnormal menstruation, and a reduced bone mineral density. Low energy availability, they reported, is linked to the other two factors and can occur in either the presence or absence of disordered eating. It can result from low calorie intake or from expending an excessive amount of energy through exercise. According to Matzkin and colleagues, women who compete in endurance sports that value leanness are especially vulnerable to the female athlete triad (424-431). Female distance runners are certainly prone to developing the triad, as they strive to maintain an ideal runner's physique. The research has shown a relatively high prevalence of the female athlete triad among women who run. In a study of 44 female endurance runners, Pollock et al. found that 15.9 percent of them displayed all three of the factors associated with the female athlete triad. Shockingly, 34.2 percent of the women suffered from low bone mineral density in the lumbar spine region, with 33 percent of them having osteoporosis in the radius (418). It is clear that the female athlete triad is common among women who run. To maintain their health and wellbeing, women who run must be mindful of their risk for the female athlete triad and take steps to ensure that they are eating properly and consuming enough nutrients to sustain their training. A future chapter will discuss nutritional guidelines for female runners, but those who are experiencing disordered eating patterns or abnormal menstruation and bone mineral density should seek treatment from a sports medicine doctor or a nutritionist who can help them to develop a healthy eating plan and treat any symptoms of the female athlete triad. Some women might also benefit from working with a mental health practitioner to resolve any pathological body image concerns or disordered eating behaviors.

The Undeniable Benefits of Running for Women

Female runners face several challenges, but staying committed to running offers a plethora of benefits for women. Perhaps the greatest benefit of running is that it provides women with an outlet for stress and frustration. After a long day of working, tending to children, and completing household chores, running relieves stress and creates a feeling of relaxation and wellbeing. Women who feel like they are struggling to balance the demands of work, home, and family can find relief in running, and use their daily run as a time just for themselves.

The stress relief associated with running can improve mental health among female runners. In a review of numerous studies, Teychenne found that vigorous physical activity reduced the risk of depression more than lower intensity physical activity did (397). Women who run and compete in races may therefore be less likely to suffer from feelings of depression, as training often requires running at a vigorous pace, and running in general is more vigorous than most other forms of physical activity.

Running also provides physical health benefits for women. It's no secret that exercise makes for a healthy heart, and running can be especially beneficial for a woman's cardiovascular system, because it can raise levels of healthy HDL cholesterol. Williams found that women who ran longer distances had significantly higher levels of HDL cholesterol ("High-Density Lipoprotein Cholesterol" 1298). Similarly, running can also reduce the need for medications that control high blood pressure and high LDL cholesterol, especially at fast paces. In another study, Williams found that women who typically ran faster than a pace of 8 minutes per mile were significantly less likely to need medications to lower cholesterol or blood pressure when compared to women who ran at a pace of slower than 11 minutes per mile ("Relationship of Running Intensity" 1740). With the rising costs of healthcare and prescription drugs, this benefit is especially important for women who run.

Beyond its effects on heart health, running has the potential to reduce a woman's risk for developing breast cancer. Gilliland found that both Hispanic and non-Hispanic White women who engaged in vigorous physical activity were less likely to develop breast cancer, even after controlling for outside factors such as body mass and calorie intake (442). Running can certainly be considered a vigorous form of exercise, so it would be reasonable to conclude that it can protect women from developing breast cancer. Wu et al. demonstrated that running could reduce the risk of breast cancer, finding that every hour per week of running at 6 miles per hour reduced breast cancer risk by 3 percent (869). Based on the results of this research, it seems that women who train intensely for long distance races such as the marathon or the half marathon are especially protected from breast cancer, as they are likely to train for upwards of three or four hours per week.

Running can also help women to burn fat, especially in the abdominal area. Most people have heard that excess abdominal fat is associated with health issues, so the fat-reducing effect of running can protect women from diseases. The high-intensity interval running that many athletes do when training for races is particularly effective in melting away belly fat. Hazell found that after women completed sprint interval training three times per week for 6 weeks, they lost an average of 8 percent of their body fat mass, and their waist sizes decreased by 3.5 percent (944). Interval training workouts will be discussed in a later chapter, as they are an integral part of training for runners. Women who include this type of workout in their training will not only experience faster race times; they can also expect their health to improve, as evidenced by the research linking interval training to decreased body fat.

Similar to its relationship with lower levels of body fat, running has also been shown to reduce age-related weight gain among women. A recent study involving over 40,000 women found that age-related increases in body mass index (BMI) were lowest among women who ran, on average, more than 32 kilometers per week, which is the equivalent of about 19 miles. The study also indicated that among women under the age of 45, running at least 40 kilometers per week, equal to 24 miles, was associated with a smaller waist size (Williams and Satariano, 1370). Based on the research, it is safe to say that women who run tend to stay lean and fit throughout the course of their lives.

Beyond the general health and fitness benefits that most women experience, running can offer advantages to mothers and mothers-to-be. Mascio et al. found that women who engaged in aerobic exercise three to four times per week during pregnancy were significantly less likely to develop gestational diabetes or high blood pressure than women in a control group were. In addition, aerobic exercise was found to be safe for pregnant women, as those who exercised had the same risk of preterm delivery and giving birth to low weight babies as women in the control group did (561). Running during pregnancy could also prevent women from gaining an unhealthy amount of weight. In a review of 11 different studies, researchers found that women who engaged in aerobic exercise during pregnancy gained about seven pounds less than women in a control group did (Lamina and Agbanusi, 62). The relationship between aerobic exercise and reduced weight gain during pregnancy is important for a woman's health, because research has shown that women who gain an excessive amount of weight during pregnancy are at an increased risk for being overweight or obese later in life (Mamun et al., 1336). Because running is a form of aerobic exercise, women who keep up with running during pregnancy can experience a variety of health benefits, including maintenance of a healthy weight, reduced risk of gestational diabetes, and decreased incidence of high blood pressure. Women who run after giving birth can also expect to experience benefits, as Tenforde et al. found that there were lower rates of postpartum depression among breastfeeding women who ran, compared to women who did not engage in any running after giving birth (172).

Lowered rates of postpartum depression are just one of the many benefits that female runners experience. The aforementioned research indicates that running is associated with a variety of positive outcomes for women, and these are substantial enough to increase a woman's life expectancy. Schnohr found that over the course of a 35-year period, female joggers were 46 percent less likely to die, and they had an increased life expectancy of 5.6 years (683). Female runners can expect to enjoy a long, healthy life if they stay committed to running and maintaining a nutritious diet. This benefit makes training worth the time and effort.

In the chapters that follow, learn about the best way to train for various different races, so you, too, can enjoy the health benefits associated with running. The training regimens discussed here are designed for intermediate level runners. The 5K training plan is best suited for women who have been casually running 5K races or consistently running at least three days per week. In order to keep up with the 5K training plan, you must be able to run at least four miles without stopping. If you have not built your fitness up to this level yet, you should consult a beginner's training guide or spend some time increasing your endurance with a walk/jog plan so you can work your way up to running four miles at once. The training plans for longer distance races, including the 10K, half marathon, and marathon, require a higher level of fitness and endurance. It is expected that women utilizing these training guides have been consistently running four to five days per week, averaging at least 20 miles per week. In some cases, women may start with the shorter distances and work their way up. For example, a woman who has been running 5K races might decide to move up to running 10Ks, or a woman who has already mastered the half marathon distance might decide she is ready to increase her training volume to prepare for a marathon. Ultimately, following these training routines should help you to improve your performance and become a stronger, faster runner. Keep in mind that the author of this book is an experienced runner but is not a medical professional. If you have questions about medical issues, such as whether or not you are healthy enough to train for long distance races, or how to treat running injuries, you should consult with a sports medicine doctor, physical therapist, or other qualified healthcare provider. You should not substitute the advice in this book for consultation with a licensed medical provider if such consultation is warranted.

Chapter 2: Mastering the 5K as a Woman

The 5K run is the first step into the world of distance running. Equivalent to 3.1 miles, a 5K is long enough to test your grit but not as daunting as longer races like the half marathon or marathon can be. Whether you live in a big city or a small town, you can probably find a 5K race near you. If you are new to the world of 5K racing, the training outline that follows will provide you with a guide to get started. It is also useful for experienced runners who want to ensure that their training is as effective as possible.

Timing Your Training for Your Best Race

Even if you are an experienced 5K runner, you cannot expect to run your best race possible if you don't commit enough time to your training. If you sign up for a race with only a few weeks' notice, you won't have time to adequately prepare, and you probably won't be happy with your performance on race day. If you want to leave yourself enough time to train for your fastest 5K, you should allow yourself at least two months for training. Two months provides you with enough time to build up your speed and endurance, while also tapering your training during the week of the race so you are fresh on race day.

Once you decide you want to run a 5K, perform an Internet search of local races, being cognizant of race dates so you have ample time to train. Once you select a race, plan to begin your training two months prior to the race. As the weeks progress, you can build up your weekly running mileage by about 10 percent per week. In the two weeks leading up to the big race, scale back your running, and leave yourself with two full days off from running immediately before the race. You might be tempted to squeeze in one last workout before race day, but intense running done too close to your 5K race will leave you with sore muscles and heavy legs on race day and will probably have a negative impact on your performance. In the two days immediately prior to your race, enjoy a leisurely walk outside, and so some light stretching exercises to relax your muscles.

Properly timing rest days throughout your training is also an integral part of being successful as a female 5K runner. After running intense workouts, your muscles need time to rest and recover, and running hard workouts back-to-back can result in overtraining and injuries. The day after a long run or a hard workout, allow yourself an easy day for recovery. You might choose to run just two to three miles at a slow pace on these days. Once per week, take the day completely off from running. You can engage in some light exercise, such as stretching or walking around the block, but avoid doing anything strenuous. When you give your body time for rest, it is better prepared to tackle the intense workouts that eventually will make you a faster 5K runner. Allowing yourself a break also makes it easier for you to balance running with other commitments, such as parenting, working, and managing your home life.

Building Endurance to Conquer the Race

Running a 5K does require some speed, but it is also important to increase your endurance if you want to run your best race. Your muscles and cardiorespiratory system are likely to become fatigued after running a 5K at maximal speed, but endurance training can habituate your body to prolonged periods of intense physical activity. This means that you must consistently run more than three miles at once during training. Plan to include a weekly long run in your training regimen. In the first week of training, this long run might only be four miles, but as you progress toward weeks four through six of training, your longer run should be closer to six or seven miles. Come race day, running only 5K, which is slightly over three miles, will feel easy compared to your long runs.

You can also build endurance by tacking extra mileage onto your harder workouts. For example, if you run an intense track workout, add a two-mile cool down at the end to increase your mileage for the day. Or, you might choose to sandwich a three-mile up-tempo run between a two mile warmup and cool down, bringing your total distance up to seven miles for the day. These types of workouts train your body to keep moving after enduring the stress of an intense effort, which can be especially useful in the latter portion of a 5K when your body begins to tire considerably. Incorporate one workout of this type per week, in addition to your weekly long run, and you will build up enough endurance to thrive on race day.

Hill workouts can also be an effective tool for building your endurance. Barnes et al. conducted a study with 20 experienced runners and found that five different types of hill training workouts, performed for six weeks, improved 5K times by an average of 2 percent (639). Using these study results, if your 5k time is currently at 20 minutes, running hill workouts throughout the course of your training could drop your time to 19:36. Smashing the 20-minute 5K barrier is certainly a monumental accomplishment in the arena of women's running. There are numerous ways to build hill workouts into your routine. Map out a course with several rolling hills, and increase your pace as you charge up each hill. Or, head to a steep hill in town; sprint up the hill, and jog down, repeating this process 10 to 20 times. Add this type of workout to your weekly routine, and you are sure to see benefits in your 5K performance.

Top 5K Speed Workouts for Women

Mastering endurance is an important part of 5K training, but to truly take your performance to the next level, you must incorporate weekly speed workouts into your routine. Once you determine your goal 5k pace, you will know how fast you need to run your speed workouts. You can search the Internet for a race pace calculator that will tell you how fast your pace per mile would be for your goal 5k time. For example, if your goal 5K time is 21 minutes, you can use a race pace calculator to determine that this is equivalent to a pace of 6:45 per mile. You will run some speed workouts at 5K pace, while you will run others slightly faster to push your body harder. To determine your ideal pace for faster speed workouts, first run a one-mile time trial at maximal effort, and pace your most intense workouts based on your mile time.

One effective speed workout for 5K runners is 400-meter repeats run at your best mile pace. For instance, if your best mile time is 6 minutes, you would run your 400-meter repeats in 1:30. If your best mile time is 8 minutes, your 400-meter repeat time would be 2 minutes. You can start with eight repeats, but ideally, you need to work your way up to 12 repeats, which would total three miles and be comparable to your 5K race distance. Run a one-lap jog around the track between each repeat for recovery. Running 12 fast 400-meter repeats will help you to improve your 5K time, because you will be training your body to run at a highly intense effort for a distance that is equivalent to the length of your race.

Half-mile, or 800-meter repeats run at your goal race pace are also an effective option for speed training. If your goal race pace were 6:45 per mile like discussed above, you would aim to run your 800-meter repeats in 3:22 each. You can start with an easier number of repeats, such as four to six at the beginning of your training, but by the end, you should be running eight 800-meter repeats, with a two-minute walk or jog between each repeat. By running eight repeats, your total volume of work at race pace exceeds the actual distance of your race, to compensate for the fact that you are taking a brief break between repeats. On race day, after habituating your body to running for a total of four miles at your desired race pace, you should ideally be able to power through the entire race at this speed.

Interval training is just as important as running repeats if you want to improve your 5K performance, and the research has proven its benefits. Denadai found that when runners completed interval training twice weekly for four weeks, their 5K running times improved significantly (737). Choose interval workouts for some of your weekly speed training sessions to reap these benefits. When training for a 5K, you might do a 20-minute interval-training workout. Warm up for five minutes, and then spend the next 20 minutes alternating between running for three minutes at the maximum speed you can maintain and jogging for two minutes to recover. Then, cool down with five minutes of jogging. This sort of workout improves your running performance and is convenient for busy women, because it only requires a total commitment of 30 minutes of your limited free time. Interval workouts are perfect for those chaotic days when you only have a narrow window of time to train, and when combined with the other workouts discussed here, they can help you to reach your 5K goals.

Sample Training Plan

Sunday	Monday	Tuesday	Wednesday	Thursday	Friday	Saturday
4 miles @ comfortable pace	Easy 2-mile run	20-minute interval run	Rest Day	4 by 400-meter repeats	Easy 3-mile run	3-mile run with hills
5 miles @ comfortable pace	Easy 2-mile run	25-minute interval run	Rest Day	5 by 400-meter repeats	Easy 3-mile run	3-mile run with hills
5 miles @ comfortable pace	Easy 2-mile run	25-minute interval run	Rest Day	6 by 400-meter repeats	Easy 3-mile run	4-mile run with hills
6 miles @ comfortable pace	Easy 2-mile run	30-minute interval run	Rest Day	4 by 800-meter repeats	Easy 3-mile run	4-mile run with hills
6 miles @ comfortable pace	Easy 2-mile run	30-minute interval run	Rest Day	6 by 800-meter repeats	Easy 3-mile run	5-mile run with hills
7 miles @ comfortable pace	Easy 2-mile run	30-minute interval run	Rest Day	8 by 800-meter repeats	Easy 3-mile run	5-mile run with hills
5 miles @ comfortable pace	Easy 2-mile run	25-minute interval run	Rest Day	8 by 800-meter repeats	Easy 3-mile run	3-mile run with hills
4 miles @ comfortable pace	Easy 2-mile run	20-minute interval run	Rest Day	Rest Day	Rest Day	Race Day

Chapter 3: How to Run Your Fastest 10K

The 10K is the perfect race for a woman who wants the challenge of a longer race but perhaps cannot commit to the more rigorous training required for a full or half marathon. The 10K will challenge your body to maintain a swift pace over a longer distance, but you can expect your speed to be about 15 to 20 seconds per mile slower than during a 5K. Even if you are not an experienced 5K runner, this training plan will guide you in the right direction.

Increasing Your Training Volume with Ease

Maybe you've met all of your 5K goals and want to move onto something else, or perhaps you are just interested in longer distances. Whatever your reason for competing in a 10K, racing this distance will require you to increase your training volume to prepare for its length. Don't worry; you won't have to double your weekly running mileage, but you will have to increase the length of your longer runs and run longer repeats on your speed workout days. You still need one day off from running per week and one especially easy day with just a two or three-mile run, but your overall mileage most days should be higher than your mileage during 5K training. If you are brand new to the world of running, you can prep for a 10K by first building up some base mileage before diving into 10K training.

To build up your distance, increase your mileage by about 10 percent a week until you reach your peak distance about two to three weeks before race day. For example, if you were running 25 miles per week training for a 5k, bump it up to 27-28 miles for a week or two, and then bump it up to 30-31 miles per week. Keep increasing your mileage until you reach your peak, which should be around 35 miles per week. The research supports increasing mileage in order to become a more accomplished 10K runner; Bale et al. found that elite 10K runners ran more miles per week than less adept 10K runners did (172).

There are several ways to add volume to your training when preparing for a 10K, and the most obvious way is to increase the length of your weekly long run. You were probably running six to seven miles for your longest run when training for a 5K, but for 10K training, your long run should increase to eight to 10 miles. Come race day, running a 10K, which is slightly over six miles, will feel simple compared to your long run. If you are accustomed to training for 5K races or you have never run longer distances, you might need to start out with a five or six-mile run and increase the distance by about half of a mile each week until you reach the desired eight to 10-mile long run. You can run at a comfortable pace; speed is not as important as familiarizing your body with the stress of running longer distances, so you will be able to endure six miles of hard running on race day. Strive to increase your long run all the way to 10 miles if you want to run your best possible 10K.

You can also add distance by adding relatively long warm-ups and cooldowns to your speed workouts. Prior to a track workout, warm up with a two-mile jog and finish with a cooldown of the same distance. In addition, you can increase the distance of one of your easy runs. Instead of running just two or three miles, head out for an easy run of five or six miles. Be sure to keep the pace slow and comfortable so your body can still recover from your harder workouts.

Intense Speed Workouts to Prepare for the 10k

The 10k requires a higher level of endurance than the 5K does, but you still need to incorporate some intense speed work into your routine, to help you maintain a brisk pace on race day. Head to the track and perform mile repeats to increase your speed. Repeats of this length are long enough to require endurance but short enough that you can still put forth an intense effort without tiring too quickly. Warm up with a one-mile jog, and then run four repeats with a one-lap recovery jog between each one. Run your repeats at the fastest pace you can sustain for one-mile to help you increase your speed. Cool down with another one-mile jog, and your total distance for the day will be right around seven miles. As your training progresses, you can boost your cooldown to two miles to add distance, as previously discussed.

Interval running is another form of speed work that is ideal for 10-k runners. Just like with the 5k, interval running is an important part of training for a 10k. You can work intervals into a six-mile run; use the first mile for a warm-up, and make the last mile your cooldown. While running the four miles in the middle, alternate three minutes at 10k race pace with two miles of easy recovery jogging. As your fitness increases throughout the course of your training, you can run four minutes at 10k race pace and one minute at a slow jog.

You can also incorporate some speed work into a standard run. For instance, if you plan to go out and run five miles, you can throw in a few sprints throughout the course of your run to increase the intensity. Or, just like with 5k training, you can map out a course with some hills, and sprint up all of the hills, but maintain a comfortable pace throughout the rest of the course. Another option for adding in speed work is starting your run at a slow, comfortable pace, and slowly increasing your speed each mile, so you finish at 10K race pace or faster for the final mile.

Tempo Runs: The Key to 10K Success

Most of the training workouts discussed here have focused on either speed or distance, but the tempo run combines these two areas, training your body to maintain an intense speed over long distances. A tempo run isn't as fast as true speed work, such as mile repeats, but it can certainly help you to run a faster 10K. Run your tempo run at the fastest pace you can maintain for one hour. It isn't an all-out effort, but it is noticeably faster than an easy run or a long run. When running at a tempo run pace, talking should be very difficult. You might be able to mutter a few words here and there, but generally, you should be working hard enough that you would rather not carry on a conversation.

Hanc of *Runner's World* has written about the benefits of tempo runs. As he explained, a tempo run trains your body to utilize oxygen efficiently and manage the metabolic byproducts of faster running. When you run at a tempo pace, your muscles become acidic, which causes fatigue. With tempo pace training, your muscles adapt and become less acidic, which enables you to keep running at a fast pace for longer. Hanc recommends that 10K runners complete tempo runs of four to six miles in length at about 15 to 20 seconds per mile slower than their 10K pace. So, if your goal pace for your 10K is 7 minutes per mile, run your tempo workout at 7:15 to 7:20 per mile. Warm up with a one-mile jog, then run at your tempo pace for four to six miles, and cool down with another one-mile jog. Do this sort of workout at least every other week throughout the course of your training.

Sample Training Plan

Sunday	Monday	Tuesday	Wednesday	Thursday	Friday	Saturday
6 miles @ comfortable pace	Easy 2-mile run	5-mile interval workout	Rest Day	4-mile tempo run	Easy 5-mile run	Easy 3-mile run
6 miles @ comfortable pace	Easy 2-mile run	4 by 1 mile repeats	Rest Day	5-mile run with hills	Easy 5-mile run	Easy 3-mile run
7 miles @ comfortable pace	Easy 2-mile run	5-mile tempo run	Rest Day	6-mile interval run	Easy 5-mile run	Easy 3-mile run
7 miles @ comfortable pace	Easy 2-mile run	4 by 1 mile repeats	Rest Day	6-mile run with one 30-second sprint per mile	Easy 5-mile run	Easy 3-mile run
8 miles @ comfortable pace	Easy 2-mile run	6-mile tempo run	Rest Day	6-mile interval run	Easy 6-mile run	Easy 3-mile run
8 miles @ comfortable pace	Easy 3-mile run	4 by 1 mile repeats	Rest Day	6-mile interval run	Easy 6-mile run	Easy 3-mile run
9 miles @ comfortable pace	Easy 3-mile run	6-mile run with hills	Rest day	6-mile tempo run	Easy 6-mile run	Easy 3-mile run
9 miles @ comfor	Easy 3-mile run	4 by 1 mile	Rest Day	6-mile run	Easy 6-	Easy 3-mile run

table pace		repeats		with hills	mile run	
10 miles @ comfortable pace	Easy 3-mile run	6-mile tempo run	Rest Day	6-mile interval run	Easy 6-mile run	Easy 3-mile run
10 miles @ comfortable pace	Easy 3-mile run	6-mile run with hills	Rest Day	6-mile run with one 30-second sprint per mile	Easy 6-mile run	Easy 3-mile run
8 miles @ comfortable pace	Easy 2-mile run	5-mile interval run	Rest Day	5-mile tempo run	Easy 6-mile run	Easy 3-mile run
7 miles @ comfortable pace	Easy 2-mile run	5-mile tempo run	Easy 4-mile run	Rest Day	Rest Day	Race Day

Chapter 4: Simple Half Marathon Training for Women

The half marathon is the entry-level race for runners who are interested in ultra-endurance events. While this 13.1 mile event does require a rigorous training regimen, preparing for a half is not as onerous as accepting the challenge of running a full marathon. The half is the perfect distance for women who want to put their endurance to the test, and most who opt to train for this race have at least a year or two of experience competing in shorter races. Some women will use the half marathon as a stepping stone to running a full marathon; others will fall in love with this distance and choose to max out at 13.1 miles. No matter what camp you fall into, there are several keys to running your best half marathon.

Making a Time Commitment

As you would probably expect, training for a half marathon requires a considerably greater time commitment than training for a 5K or 10K race. Not only will your overall training volume increase considerably when preparing for a half marathon; you will also need to incorporate a run of up to 15 miles into your weekly routine. Some half marathoners are able to meet their goal race time with a long run of 10-12 miles, but if you want to truly reach your full potential, you should aim for your long run to be right around 15 miles. A long run of this distance will prepare your muscles to fight through the fatigue and maintain a swift pace in the final miles of the half marathon. You can expect to spend two or two-and- a-half hours on your weekly long run; if you opt for a shorter run of 10-12 miles, expect to spend an hour-and- a-half out running. Either way, the time commitment is significant.

You should also expect your speed workouts to be longer with half marathon training. For instance, instead of running 400-meter repeats, you will probably run two-mile repeats throughout the course of your training. Once you add in a warm-up and cool down, you can expect workouts of this nature to take slightly over an hour to complete. In order to make time for this type of training, you might have to give up some activities, such as going to happy hour with friends or watching one of your favorite TV shows every evening. You will probably struggle to keep up with training if you are balancing other commitments, such as taking college classes or maintaining part-time work outside of your normal nine to five job, so be sure that you have room in your schedule for the rigorous training that running a fast half marathon requires. You will have easier days in your training in which you only run for about a half hour, but most days you can expect your training to require 45 minutes to an hour of commitment, with about two days per week of workouts that last over an hour, including your two-hour long run day.

Between adding distance to your long runs and increasing the volume of your speed work, you can expect your total weekly distance to creep up to 40 to 50 miles during the peak of your half marathon training. It is also important to note that when training for a half marathon, you typically need to allow three to four months for your training; you also must permit time for a four-week taper, during which you scale back your training to prepare your body for an optimal performance on race day. You will spend the beginning month of your training building up your mileage, peak for the middle month or two, and then reduce your mileage and intensity in the last month leading up to your race. This differs considerably from 5k or 10k training, during which you might train for two months and cut back your training the week before the race.

You can manage this rigorous training regimen with careful planning and preparation. Most half marathoners choose to save their long runs for the weekends. Head out first thing on a Saturday morning to get the long run out of the way so you can enjoy the rest of the day with your family. If you are a mother, the only thing you will miss is breakfast and cartoons with the kids. You might want to plan your more lengthy speed workouts for days of the week when you aren't as busy. For instance, pick a day of the week when you don't have any evening meetings to attend or sports practices where you have to shuttle your kids, and do your longest workout on this day. You might also want to save your easier runs for the busiest days of your week. Some women find it helpful to do an easy three or four-mile run on Monday evening to ease into the work week and recover from a weekend full of harder, longer runs. However you choose to plan your training, preparing for a half marathon is doable for busy women who are willing to make it a priority.

Choosing the Perfect Goal Time and Training to Achieve It

Before beginning your half marathon training, it is important to set a goal time so you know how fast to run during your training. Generally, your half marathon pace will be about 30 to 45 seconds per mile slower than your 5K time. Keep this in mind when setting a goal time, and use an online race pace calculator to determine what your finish time will be.

Throughout the course of your training, it is important to do some running at your race pace to accustom your body to this speed. One workout that can acquaint your body with your half marathon pace is warming up with a one-mile jog, running at half marathon race pace for six miles, and cooling down with an easy mile. Do this work out several times throughout the course of your training so your body will be comfortable with your pace on race day.

Another way to familiarize your body with your half marathon pace is to sign up for a 10K about a month before race day. Use this race as a dress rehearsal; go to bed at the same time you will the night before you half marathon and wake up at the same time in the morning, and eat the same thing for breakfast that you intend to eat on race day. Run the 10K at the same pace you have decided upon for your half marathon, and see how your body feels. Your effort during the 10K should feel comfortably hard; similar to a tempo run, you might be able to utter a few words but will be too fatigued to carry on a conversation.

Training at a brisk pace is also a key component of achieving a fast half marathon time, as the research has linked an increased training pace to a faster half marathon finish. Specifically, women who run faster during training tend to have less fat in their upper bodies, which researchers have found is associated with better performance in the half marathon (Knechtle et al, 158). Friedrich et al. also found that women who ran faster during training and had lower body fat percentages performed better in the half marathon (10). Therefore, it appears that you can increase your chances of achieving your goal race pace by keeping most of your training runs brisk. This sort of training can help you to stay lean, which is associated with faster race times.

Workouts that Combine Speed with Endurance

The half marathon truly is the perfect combination of speed and endurance; your pace for this race is noticeably slower than for shorter distances like the 5K, but you must run faster than you typically would for a run of such a long distance. After all, during training, most of your longer runs are at a slow, comfortable pace. With your half marathon training, you must teach your body to maintain speed over distance. Most of your workouts should be longer distance runs into which your incorporate some variation of speed work.

One such run is a longer interval run. With the 5K and the 10K, you might have done interval runs of between two to six miles, but for the half marathon, you can bump your interval workout up to eight to ten miles. Throughout the course of the run, alternate three minutes at a brisk pace with two minutes of a slower recovery jog. Another similar workout involves warming up for a mile, running five to seven miles at your half marathon pace, and then cooling down with a one-mile jog.

Tempo runs are also of benefit to half marathon runners. As discussed in the chapter on training for a 10K, tempo runs help your body to become more efficient at utilizing the metabolic byproducts of faster running, so your muscles don't fatigue as quickly. Incorporating several tempo runs of seven to nine miles throughout the course of your training can help you to maintain your speed in the latter portion of a half marathon.

You can also head to the track for two-mile repeats to build up your speed. After a one-mile warm up, run three 2-mile repeats at your best 10K race pace, each separated by an 800-meter recovery jog. Cool down with another mile run, and your total distance for this workout will be nine miles. This workout boosts endurance because of its relatively long total distance but also improves speed because the repeats are run at your 10K pace, which is brisk but perhaps not as strenuous as the pace at which you run shorter repeats, such as 800-meters or 400-meters.

Another workout that boosts your endurance but also prepares you to run swiftly on race day is a long run in which you run the second half faster than the first half. Choose an eight to 10-mile course, and run the first half at a comfortable pace. Note how long it takes you to run the first half, and aim to shave off two to five minutes during the second half. This workout is ideal for half-marathon training because it teaches your body to run at a fast pace despite being tired. This is especially important in the latter portion of a half marathon when fatigue makes you want to slow your pace, but you have to stay strong and stick to your goal race pace. Much like the other workouts that combine speed and endurance, this one incorporates speed work into a long run. This sort of training is integral to your half marathon preparation, and you should run this type of workout at least five times throughout the course of your training.

Sample Training Plan

Sunday	Monday	Tuesday	Wednesday	Thursday	Friday	Saturday
8 miles @ comfortable pace	Easy 3-mile run	6-mile interval run	Rest Day	6-mile run with second half faster than first	Easy 5-mile run	Easy 3-mile run
9 miles @ comfortable pace	Easy 3-mile run	6-mile interval run	Rest Day	7-mile run with final 3 miles faster than first 4	Easy 6-mile run	Easy 3-mile run
10 miles @ comfortable pace	Easy 3-mile run	7-mile tempo run	Rest Day	8-mile run with second half faster than first	Easy 6-mile run	Easy 3-mile run
11 miles @ comfortable pace	Easy 3-mile run	8-mile interval run	Rest Day	8-mile run with second half faster than first	Easy 6-mile run	Easy 4-mile run
12 miles @ comfortable pace	Easy 3-mile run	8-mile tempo run	Rest Day	8-mile run with second half faster than first	Easy 6-mile run	Easy 4-mile run

13 miles @ comfortable pace	Easy 3-mile run	3 by 2-mile repeats @ 10K pace	Rest Day	9-mile interval run	Rest Day	10K race @ half marathon pace
14 miles @ comfortable pace	Easy 3-mile run	6 mile run @ half marathon pace	Rest Day	9-mile interval run	Easy 6-mile run	Easy 4-mile run
15 miles @ comfortable pace	Easy 3-mile run	8 mile run with second half faster than first	Rest Day	8-mile tempo run	Easy 6-mile run	Easy 4-mile run
12 miles @ comfortable pace	Easy 3-mile run	6-mile run @ half marathon pace	Rest Day	9-mile interval run	Easy 6-mile run	Easy 4-mile run
10 miles @ comfortable pace	Easy 3-mile run	3 by 2-mile repeats @ 10K pace	Rest Day	10-mile interval run	Easy 6-mile run	Easy 4-mile run
8 miles @ comfortable pace	Easy 3-mile run	6-mile run @ half marathon pace	Rest Day	8-mile tempo run	Easy 5-mile run	Easy 4-mile run
7 miles @ comfortable pace	Easy 3-mile run	6-mile run with second half faster than first	Easy 2-mile run	Rest Day	Rest Day	Race Day

Chapter 5: How Women Should Train for a Marathon

The marathon is perhaps the most revered race in the world of distance running. At 26.2 miles, this race is no small feat. Most women who train for marathons are seasoned runners who have been running shorter distances for several years, or perhaps they have been slowly working their way up to being able to run this lengthy race. If you are ready to take the plunge and run a full marathon, you will have to be prepared to spend seven to 10 hours per week training, and you can expect your weekly running mileage to peak around 50. The fastest marathon runners tend to log even higher mileage. In a study of elite Norwegian marathon runners, Enoksen et al. found that the average weekly running distance for this group was 186.6 kilometers, which is equivalent to 112 miles of running per week (273). As a recreational marathoner, it is not necessary for you to engage in such a high volume of training, but you should expect to run a considerable number of miles each week, and you might have to increase your training mileage with each subsequent race if you want to continue to improve your marathon times. You also must be able to commit at least four months to your training for the best results. Putting adequate time and effort into training is imperative if you want to complete a full marathon, as the research has shown that individuals who drop out of the marathon are typically ill prepared for the race (Yeung et al., 170).

Garnering Support from Loved Ones

Because preparing for a marathon is so undeniably rigorous, your training will need to be a priority, and you might have to make sacrifices in other areas of your life in order to stay committed to it. It is important to gather support from your family if you want to be successful. Sit down with your spouse or partner and explain your goals and your reasons for running to ensure that you have his or her support. Your partner might have to take on more of the day-to-day chores around the home to enable you to complete your training. For example, if you typically share the household chores equally, your partner might have to take over some of your duties temporarily. Or, if you typically shuffle the kids to and from soccer practice, your partner might need to take on this duty so you can fit in a workout during this time. While the demands of training are temporary, it is important for your family to understand the commitment you have made, so they can be helpful throughout the process, without building any resentment toward you. Training for a marathon is tough, and if you have a supportive family cheering you on, you will have an easier time staying committed.

The literature has reinforced the importance of family support for marathon runners. Goodsell and Harris have researched the impact of marathon training on family life, and they found that family members generally worked together to manage the commitment of someone in the family running a marathon (88). They also discovered that runners found spousal support to be important and valuable, and they used strategies such as planning schedules with their spouses and asking their spouses for help around the house. Women, in particular, asked their husbands to watch the children or assist with housework while they ran, and the husbands were generally compliant with these requests; some even offered to help (89-97). It appears that coordinating schedules and dividing tasks so that you have enough time to run can help you to stay committed to your training while also meeting the demands of family life. Obtaining support from your family and making a plan for completing household tasks will prevent you from falling off track with your marathon training. Having emotional support from your spouse or partner is also critical, because marathon training is a daunting, albeit rewarding, task.

Mastering the Long Run for Marathon Success

Family support is probably the most important when it comes to your weekly long run, because mastering it is the number one key to marathon success. Some weeks, your long run will only be 10-12 miles, but as your training progresses, it will peak around 24 miles to prepare you for race day. For most women, running this long of a distance will require them to be away from their families for at least three hours. This is why many marathoners schedule their long runs for a Saturday or Sunday morning. Pencil in the long run on your schedule and stay committed to it, and you will be much more likely to meet your marathon goals.

Develop a plan of action so you know how you will divide household responsibilities during the weekend so you still have time for your run.

Once you make a plan for committing to your weekly long run, you then must acclimate your body to the stress of running longer distances. Slowly increase your mileage for the first few weeks of your training. You can begin by running 10 miles for your weekly long run. Then, bump it up to 11 miles, and then 12. Keep moving the distance up by a mile or two every week until you reach 16 miles. Then, back off for a week and go back down to 12 miles to give your body a chance to recover from the effort of running a 16 miler. The next week, increase your distance to 18 miles. The following week, cut the long run back to 12 miles again. Continue this alternating pattern until a month before the race, when you will run your longest run of 24-26 miles. In the weeks that follow, cut your long run back to 12 miles, then to 10 miles, where it will stay until the week before race day. The high mileage training required for marathon running strains the body, but by alternating between a significantly long run and a more moderate distance run in this way, you protect yourself from injury.

The long run is non-negotiable for marathon success. Your body simply will not be able to endure the stress of running 26.2 miles if you have not become accustomed to running significantly long distances. The research has supported the necessity of the long run for marathon training programs. In a study of 113 marathon participants, 58 of whom dropped out during the early miles of the race, researchers found that the longest distance covered in one training session was the factor most strongly linked to marathon completion (Yeung et al., 170).

Marathon Prep Workouts You Must Do

Mastering the long run is imperative for marathon success, but other types of workouts play an important role in preparing you for your race. One such workout is the famous Yasso 800's, which Burfoot of *Runner's World* has argued are key if you want to hit your goal time in your race ("The Real History"). As Burfoot has explained, if you want to finish a marathon in 3 hours and 30 minutes, you should be able to run 800-meter repeats in 3 minutes and 30 seconds each. Begin by running four 800-meter repeats at your goal pace toward the beginning of your training, and increase the number of repeats until you are running 10 of them two to three weeks before your race. It is not necessary to run Yasso 800's every week, but they should be interspersed throughout your training every few weeks. If you can run 10 repeats at your desired marathon pace, you should be able to reach your goal. Burfoot tested this workout with approximately 100 runners and found that it was effective for marathon paces ranging from slightly over two hours to over four hours. Regardless of your abilities, this workout will challenge you and give you an idea of how close you are to meeting your goal time in the marathon. If you notice that you are hitting a pace of three minutes and thirty-five seconds for your Yasso 800's but you hope to finish the marathon in under three hours and thirty minutes, you might have to step up your training.

The tempo run is also vital to your success as a marathoner. Start small with a tempo run of five to six miles, and work your way up to running tempo runs of 10 miles. To challenge yourself, choose a difficult course with several hills interspersed throughout for your tempo runs, especially if you know that your race course will be hilly. Each week, incorporate tempo runs with your other forms of speed work, such as repeats. To prepare for your marathon, you can run either eight one-mile repeats or four two-mile repeats at about 30 seconds faster than your marathon pace. Be sure to throw in easy runs of two to four miles or rest days after your tempo run or speed work days to give your body plenty of time to recover and prepare for your long run days.

Beyond speedier workouts, you should also be running some of your workouts at marathon race pace. Warm-up with a one-mile jog, and then run for six to eight miles at your goal marathon pace. Cool down with another one-mile jog, bringing your total to eight to 10 miles for the day. It is also beneficial to do interval workouts of the same length throughout your training. You can alternate interval workouts, tempo workouts, and workouts run at marathon pace.

Sample Training Plan

Sunday	Monday	Tuesday	Wednesday	Thursday	Friday	Saturday
10 mile @ comfortable pace	Easy 3-mile run	6-mile tempo run	Rest Day	4 Yasso 800's	4-mile easy run	6-mile Easy run
11 miles @ comfortable pace	Easy 3-mile run	6-mile run @ marathon pace	Rest Day	8 by 1-mile repeats	4-mile easy run	6-mile easy run
12 miles @ comfortable pace	Easy 3-mile run	8-mile interval run	Rest Day	4 by 2-mile repeats	4-mile easy run	6-mile easy run
14 miles @ comfortable pace	Easy 3-mile run	8-mile tempo run	Rest Day	5 Yasso 800's	4-mile easy run	6-mile easy run
16 miles @ comfortable pace	Easy 3-mile run	10-mile run @ marathon pace	Rest Day	8 by 1-mile repeats	4-mile easy run	6-mile easy run
12 miles @ comfortable pace	Easy 3-mile run	8-mile interval run	Rest Day	4 by 2-mile repeats	4-mile easy run	6-mile easy run
18 miles @ comfortable pace	Easy 3-mile run	8-mile tempo run	Rest Day	6 Yasso 800's	4-mile easy run	6-mile easy run

12 miles @ comfortable pace	Easy 3-mile run	8-mile run @ marathon pace	Rest Day	8 by 1-mile repeats	4-mile easy run	6-mile easy run
20 miles @ comfortable pace	Easy 3-mile run	8-mile interval run	Rest Day	4 by 2-mile repeats	4-mile easy run	6-mile easy run
12 miles @ comfortable pace	Easy 3-mile run	6-mile tempo run	Rest Day	8 Yasso 800's	4-mile easy run	6-mile easy run
22 miles @ comfortable pace	Easy 3-mile run	10-mile run @ marathon pace	Rest Day	8 by 1-mile repeats	4-mile easy run	6-mile easy run
12 miles @ comfortable pace	Easy 3-mile run	6-mile interval run	Rest Day	4 by 2-mile repeats	4-mile easy run	6-mile easy run
24 miles @ comfortable pace	Easy 3-mile run	8-mile tempo run	Rest Day	10 Yasso 800's	4-mile easy run	6-mile easy run
12 miles @ comfortable pace	Easy 3-mile run	6-mile run @ marathon pace	Rest Day	6 by 1-mile repeats	4-mile easy run	6-mile easy run
10 miles @ comfor	Easy 3-mile run	6-mile interval run	Rest Day	4 by 1-mile repeats	4-mile easy run	6-mile easy run

table pace						
10 miles @ comfor table pace	Easy 3-mile run	6-mile tempo run	Easy 3-mile run	Rest Day	Rest Day	Race Day

Chapter 6: Other Considerations for Female Runners

While training is important, there are additional factors that play a role in a woman's success in running. To run your best race, you must also maintain a balanced diet that provides your body with the energy and nutrients needed for peak performance. Furthermore, reaching your maximum running potential requires you to build strength and develop healthy sleep habits.

Eating for Optimal Performance

Proper nutrition is perhaps as important for female runners as training is. To fuel your training, you need to consume enough calories, as well as the proper amounts of vitamins, minerals, and macronutrients like fat, protein, and carbohydrates.

Consuming an Adequate Number of Calories

Running long distances, especially at brisk paces, burns a considerable amount of calories, and you must ensure that you calorie intake is adequate. If you are overweight, there are certainly health and performance benefits associated with weight loss, but you should not be attempting to cut calories while training for a race. Consistently operating under a calorie deficit will eventually lead to fatigue and burnout, and you won't have the energy to power through your tough workouts or your race.

Researchers have determined the ideal calorie intake for female runners. Deldicque and Francaux have asserted that female endurance runners require at minimum 45 calories per kilogram of fat-free mass per day, in addition to the number of calories burned during physical activity (1). This means that each day, for every kilogram of fat-free mass on your body, you need 45 calories, and you must add to this the number of calories you burn while running. For an example let's consider a woman who weighs 140 pounds and has 20 percent body fat. This means that 80 percent, or 112 pounds, of her body mass is fat-free. We can divide 112 by 2.2 to arrive at the equivalent weight in kilograms, which is 50.91. 50.91 multiplied by 45 is 2,290 calories per day. Let's say the woman burns an average of 350 calories per day while running, and she would need a minimum of 2,640 calories per day to support her training. This amount may seem relatively high compared to the widely recommended 2,000 calorie per day diet, and it is especially elevated when one considers the fact that some women stick to low calorie diets that provide only 1,200 to 1,500 calories per day. Regardless, this high calorie intake is necessary for women who are training for long distance races. Keep in mind that this calorie recommendation is the minimum energy requirement for runners; women who are engaging in especially intense training or preparing for longer races such as the marathon or half marathon might need even more calories per day to sustain their high activity levels.

See figure 1, which follows, for an estimate of the minimum daily calorie needs for women of various body weights, using the numbers reported by Deldicque and Francaux.

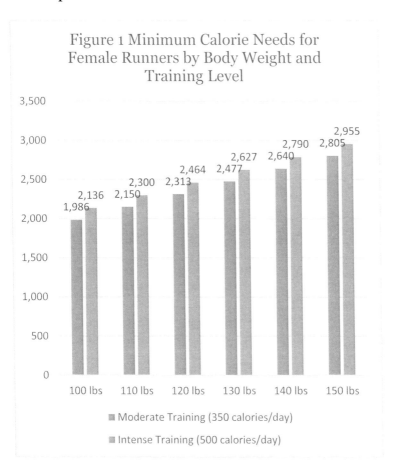

Figure 1 Minimum Calorie Needs for Female Runners by Body Weight and Training Level

The calorie needs displayed in this graph were calculated for women with 20 percent body fat. You can estimate your own calorie needs by first dividing your weight in pounds by 2.2 to arrive at your weight in kilograms. Then, to determine the percentage of your body that is comprised of fat-free mass, subtract your body fat percentage from 100. For instance,xz if you have 30 percent body fat, your body's lean mass would be 70 percent, or .70. Multiply your weight in kilograms by .70 to determine your body's total fat free mass, and then multiply this value by 45. Then, add in the number of calories you burn per day during training.

As an example, let's use a woman who weighs 170 pounds, has 30 percent body fat, and burns 350 calories per day while running. Her weight in kilograms would be 77, multiplied by .70 (her fat free mass percentage) would be 54.091. Multiply this by 45 to arrive at the number of calories she needs per kilogram of fat-free mass, and the result is 2,434 calories. Add in the 350 calories she burns while running, and her total calorie needs for the day are 2,784. Use this same formula, inputting your own weight, lean mass, and calorie burn during exercise, to determine the minimum number of calories you need per day to sustain your training.

Including Essential Vitamins and Minerals in the Diet

Sufficient calorie intake is critical for women who run, but their diets must also include adequate amounts of essential vitamins and minerals. One such mineral is iron, which Hinton has asserted plays an integral role in the performance of endurance athletes, because of its association with metabolism and oxygen transport (1012). Unfortunately, female runners are especially vulnerable to iron deficiency. In a study of marathon runners, Mettler and Zimmermann found that 25.5 percent of the women suffered from functional iron deficiency, compared to only 3.9 percent of the men (490). As DellaValle has explained, the early stages of iron deficiency can negatively affect endurance performance because of changes in muscle metabolism. As iron deficiency grows more severe, she indicated, there can be an impact on oxygen transport and oxidative capacity, which can adversely impact vO_2 max and endurance (234-235). Iron is therefore essential if you want to reach your full running potential. Include iron-rich foods such as meat, beans, and leafy greens in your diet to ensure that you get an adequate amount of this essential nutrient. If you have concerns that your iron levels might be low, consult with your doctor to have blood work done. In the case of anemia, you might need to take an iron supplement to return your iron levels to a healthy range.

The B vitamins are also critical for runners. As Woolf and Manore have explained, these vitamins are involved with energy production, the creation of new red blood cells, and the mending of damaged cells, so athletes who do not consume adequate quantities might struggle to perform high-intensity physical activity (453). Pack your diet with foods such as bananas, leafy green vegetables, whole grain breads, fortified cereals, pasta, and chicken to ensure that you are getting an ample amount of the B vitamins. You might even consider taking a supplement to provide your body with the nutrition it needs to perform optimally.

Vitamin D is particularly important to runners, because of its role in maintaining health. In fact, vitamin D can protect runners from developing illnesses that derail their training. He et al. analyzed the impact of vitamin D on upper respiratory infections in a group of endurance athletes during four months of winter training, and they found that athletes with optimal levels of vitamin D in their blood experienced fewer upper respiratory infections during the study period than individuals who were deficient in vitamin D did. Individuals with optimal vitamin D levels also experienced fewer days with upper respiratory symptoms, and their symptoms were less severe when compared to those who were deficient in vitamin D (86). In addition to keeping you free from illness, vitamin D could make you a stronger runner. Wyon analyzed the impact of a vitamin D supplement on a group of athletes and discovered that supplementation increased their muscle strength by 13 percent (279). Strengthen your own muscles by incorporating yogurt, cheese, cow's milk, almond milk, egg yolks, fortified orange juice, and fortified cereals into your diet.

Magnesium is also of benefit to women who run. As Lee has explained, multiple studies have found that magnesium exerts an effect on athletic performance (799). Specifically, Lukaski and Nielsen found that when women were deficient in magnesium, their bodies used oxygen less efficiently during aerobic exercise, and their heart rates were elevated, implying an impact on fitness level (930). It is therefore reasonable to conclude that a lack of magnesium in the diet could have a deleterious impact on your running performance. Include nuts, bananas, and vegetables such as peas and broccoli in your diet to ensure that your magnesium intake is adequate.

Eating the Right Amounts of Macronutrients

Beyond packing your diet with essential vitamins and minerals, you must ensure that you are consuming the right amount of fat, protein, and carbohydrates to energize your body for training. Most runners are aware that they need to consume a considerable amount of carbohydrates, and after reviewing the relevant research, Burke et al. have advised that athletes need to take in enough carbohydrates to fuel their training and to replenish muscle glycogen stores after exercise (15). Experts have determined a runner's carbohydrate needs based upon her body weight, and the recommendation is five to seven grams of carbohydrates per kilogram of body weight each day during lower intensity training and seven to 12 grams per kilogram of body weight during periods of moderate or high-intensity training (Burke et al., 21). Use your best judgment to determine where your carbohydrate needs fall based upon your training intensity. If you are following an intense training program such as a half marathon or marathon plan, for instance, you can expect your carbohydrate requirement to be at the higher end of the range. Recall our earlier discussion regarding converting your weight in pounds to kilograms, and you can multiply your body weight in kilograms by the appropriate number to determine your daily carbohydrate needs. For instance, a 130-pound woman weighs the equivalent of 59 kilograms. Multiply this number by five and seven, and you would conclude that this woman needs 295-413 grams of carbohydrates per day during periods of low-intensity training. Multiply it by 12, and you discover that the carbohydrate need jumps to 709 grams per day for the most intense training regimens. Consult figure 2 below for an estimation of your daily carbohydrate needs based upon weight and training status.

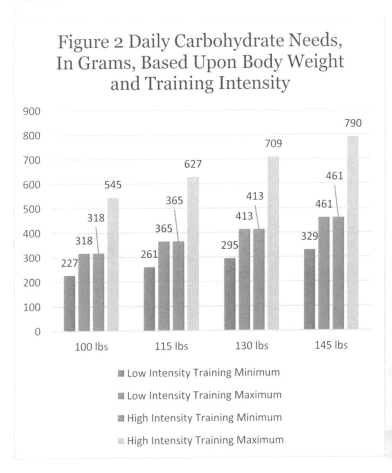

Figure 2 Daily Carbohydrate Needs, In Grams, Based Upon Body Weight and Training Intensity

■ Low Intensity Training Minimum
■ Low Intensity Training Maximum
■ High Intensity Training Minimum
■ High Intensity Training Maximum

Carbohydrates can also have an impact on performance when consumed before big races. Deldicque and Francaux have reported that female runners would benefit from "carbohydrate loading" the day before a race, which involves consuming at least eight grams of carbohydrates per pound of body weight (1). Researchers have proven this strategy to be effective. Atkinson et al. found that runners who consumed at least seven grams of carbohydrates per kilogram of body weight the day before a marathon ran significantly faster and maintained their pace more easily than competitors consuming fewer carbohydrates did (611). Fuel your body with extra carbohydrates the day before a race in addition to consuming an adequate amount of carbs throughout your training to ensure optimal performance.

Carbohydrates are a vital source of energy for runners, but fat and protein are also important. Kato et al. conducted a study on the protein needs of endurance athletes and concluded that their protein requirements far exceed those of sedentary individuals. The study team explained that endurance athletes display a higher metabolic demand for protein when training intensely, and they recommended that endurance athletes consume between 1.65 and 1.83 grams of protein per day, per kilogram of body weight, which is higher than the recommended .8 gram per kilogram of body weight recommended for the general population (7). For a woman who weighs 130 pounds, this means protein needs during bouts of heavy training would range from 97.5 to 108 grams per day.

Fat is just as important as protein. In a review of the relevant research, Venkatraman et al. reported that increasing dietary fat intake is beneficial for endurance athletes, because the research indicates that it helps to maintain the functioning of the immune system, and it can improve performance (S389). Dietary fat is especially important for female runners and can prevent them from being sidelined by injuries. In a study of women who ran at least 20 miles per week, Gerlach et al. found that those who consumed more fat were less likely to develop injuries over the course of the study. Women who became injured consumed an average of 63 grams of fat per day, whereas non-injured runners consumed 80 grams, on average (4). It is clear that women needn't worry about consuming too much fat when training for a race, and dietary fat can even help them grow into faster runners. Healthy fats, such as those found in avocados, nuts, peanut butter, and olive oil can fuel your running, and you can safely include foods high in saturated fats, such as beef and cheese, in your diet. The media often portrays saturated fat in a negative manner, linking it to heart disease and high cholesterol, but in a review of 21 studies involving over 300,000 participants, Siri-Tarino et al. found that saturated fat intake was not linked to an increased risk of heart disease (535).

Other Nutrition Tips

As the research indicates, female runners benefit from maintaining a healthy diet that provides them with an adequate intake of calories, vitamins, minerals, and macronutrients to fuel their bodies during training and competitions. Eating a balanced diet that incorporates nutrient-rich foods can enhance performance, and female runners typically need greater amounts of nutrients than their non-active counterparts do. Beyond these general guidelines for adequate dietary intake, there are specific foods that the research suggests can have an ergogenic effect of running performance. While not necessary for all runners, you can incorporate these foods into your diet, and they might just boost your performance even further. You can try some or all of these foods to determine if they are of benefit to you.

Tart cherries are one such food that might make you a better runner, and the research has proven their benefits. Levers et al. conducted an experiment to analyze the impact of tart cherries on a group of endurance athletes. They found that compared to individuals in a placebo group, those who consumed tart cherry powder for 10 days completed a half marathon run 13 percent faster, and they experienced less soreness and lower levels of inflammation following the run (7-8). In a similar study, Kuehl et al. found that runners who consumed tart cherry juice for seven days prior to and on the day of a 26.3-kilometer race experienced less pain after the event than runners in a control group did(4). You might consider making tart cherry juice or smoothies containing tart cherries a part of your daily diet. The effect of the tart cherries could prevent you from experiencing debilitating muscle soreness and could even help you run faster come race day.

Calcium-rich foods, especially dairy products, can also play an important role in your wellbeing as a female runner. Nieves et al. found that young women who ran long distances were less likely to suffer from stress fractures when they consumed more calcium-rich foods, dairy products, and skim milk. The intake of these foods was also linked to increased bone mineral density (740). If you have a history of stress fractures or a family predisposition to osteoporosis, incorporating calcium-rich foods such as milk, cheese, and yogurt in your diet can strengthen your bones and prevent you from developing a debilitating stress fracture during your training.

Beyond dairy products, you would also benefit from incorporating antioxidant-rich fruits and vegetables into your diet. You have probably heard about the health benefits associated with a type of antioxidant called polyphenols, and it is no surprise that these antioxidants can improve athletic performance. In an analysis of 14 different studies, Somerville et al. found that polyphenols supplements, when taken for at least seven days, improved athletic performance by nearly two percent (1589). Blueberries, raspberries, strawberries, blackberries, kiwi, cherries, apples, grapes, apricots, kale, peaches, and broccoli are all excellent sources of polyphenols (Manach et al., 729), and when regularly included in your diet, they could slightly enhance your performance. Even if the impact on your running performance is marginal, the inclusion of these nutrient-rich foods in your diet will provide your body with the vitamins and minerals needed for optimal functioning.

Training with Weights for Increased Strength

The majority of most training plans is comprised of running, but adding resistance training, or weight lifting, to your routine can strengthen your muscles and help them to power through races at faster speeds. Johnson et al. conducted a study with female runners, in which the women completed strength training three times per week for 10 weeks. The women who did the weight training increased their upper and lower body strength, and compared to those in a control group, their running economy improved significantly (226). The improvement in running economy that is seen with weight training is especially noteworthy. As Saunders et al. have explained, running economy is the energy requirement for a specific speed of running, and it involves the amount of oxygen the body consumes during exercise. Runners with better running economy use less energy and less oxygen for a specific speed of running when compared to less economical runners, they reported, and running economy therefore is linked to distance running performance (465).

The research has strongly supported the benefits of strength training for running economy and distance running performance. Blagrove et al. analyzed the results of 24 different studies and found that in general, strength training improves running economy and time trial performance. Blagrove and his colleagues concluded that runners would benefit from adding two or three weekly strength training sessions to their usual routines (1).

Your strength training sessions do not have to be complicated or lengthy for you to see benefits. As Blagrove at al. said, only two or three sessions per week are necessary, and you can do these sessions from your own home with free weights. Schedule your sessions prior to your run on easy days, and plan to commit 15 to 20 minutes to them. Aim to do two to three sets, each with 10 to 12 repetitions of various exercises. Strength training exercises can include biceps curls, military presses, bench presses, triceps extensions, weighted squats, lunges, pushups, and planks.

Weight training exercises that strengthen your core could be particularly beneficial if you want to become a faster runner. Sato and Mokha assessed the impact of core strength training on a group of runners. One group served as a control group, and the other group performed core exercises four times per week for six weeks. At the beginning and end of the study, both the control group and the core training group completed a 5K time trial. The individuals in the core training group improved their 5K times by an average of 47 seconds, whereas those in the control group only improved by 17 seconds (137). Incorporating several core workouts into your regular weight lifting sessions could pay off in the form of a significantly faster race time.

Maintaining Healthy Sleep Habits

Amidst all your training, it is important to take time to rest, and ensuring that you get adequate sleep will give you the energy to meet the demands of your rigorous training regimen. Lastella et al. have reported that sleep is necessary for ensuring recovery and top performance (293), but the research has shown that athletes sleep less when they are training, and less sleep is linked to fatigue on training days (Sargent et al., 1160). Being fatigued could prevent you from putting forth maximum effort into your workouts, and it is therefore critical that you consistently get an adequate amount of sleep.

Prioritize sleep by sticking to a consistent sleep schedule with an early enough bedtime to ensure adequate rest. To develop a healthy sleep rhythm, go to bed around the same time each day and awaken at the same time in the morning, even on days when you don't have to be up at a certain time for work or training. Keeping a consistent schedule makes it easier to fall asleep and stay asleep throughout the night, because your body will become accustomed to sleeping at certain times.

While the amount of sleep your body gets is important, the quality of that sleep is equally significant. If you are spending most of the night tossing and turning, or you spend hours awake in the middle of the night, your sleep won't be restorative, and you will struggle to make it through your workouts. Several factors can affect the quality of your sleep. You can promote quality sleep by maintaining a quiet, comfortable sleep environment. The temperature should be cool, and you might consider using a white noise machine to drown out environmental noise. If you find your bed or pillow to be uncomfortable or you wake up with a sore back or stiff neck, it might be time to invest in a new pillow or mattress. It is also important to avoid stimulating beverages, such as caffeinated coffee or energy drinks in the afternoon and evening, and you might even find that it is necessary to cut out caffeine altogether if you are struggling to sleep. In addition, you can prepare your body for sleep by winding down with a calming bedtime routine, such as reading for twenty minutes, and avoiding television shows, social media, and loud music in the hour before bed.

The research has supported these specific sleep hygiene methods. A recent study found that adults who surfed the Internet or played on their phones and computers before bed were more likely to suffer from insomnia. Texting on a cellphone prior to bedtime was also linked to sleeplessness (Nesdal Fossum et al., 343). In addition, researchers have discovered a relationship between temperature and sleep quality. Obradovich et al. found that higher nighttime temperatures were linked to a lack of sleep. These researchers explained that a decrease in core temperature signals the body that it is time for sleep, so temperature plays a critical role in sleep regulation (1). Finally, scientists have also uncovered a link between caffeine consumption and sleep disturbances. In an experimental study, participants consumed either caffeinated tea, caffeinated coffee, or water, and they completed a sleep questionnaire to assess their sleep quality. Study results showed that when participants consumed more caffeine, they took longer to fall asleep, slept less, and had lower sleep quality. They consumed caffeinated beverages four times per day, and their total caffeine intake ranged from 150 mg to 600 mg per day; higher caffeine intakes resulted in more sleep disturbances (Hindmarch et al., 203). It is important to be mindful of your caffeine consumption, as well as your evening electronic use and the temperature of your bedroom if you want to ensure optimal sleep quality. Making this extra effort to promote healthy sleep habits will rejuvenate your body and prepare you for tough training sessions.

Sleep is important throughout your training, but chances are that your sleep might be lacking the night before a big race. Anxiety, coupled with the need to awaken earlier than usual to eat breakfast and to get to the race for an early start time, can cut your sleep short. Try not to worry too much if you can't sleep the night before a race or just don't log as many hours as usual. The pre-race adrenaline will likely give you plenty of energy to power through your race, and you can make up for lost sleep with an afternoon nap after crossing the finish line. What is most important is getting an adequate amount of rest throughout your training, especially during the week leading up to the race, so one off night before the competition won't significantly deprive your body of the restorative sleep it needs to perform optimally.

Chapter 7: Staying the Course

Even if you're following a solid training plan and you've fine-tuned it with proper nutrition, weight training, and healthy sleep habits, there will be times when life gets in the way of your running goals. Whether it's an incapacitating injury or a busy period at work, sometimes there will be roadblocks that prevent you from sticking to your training.

Managing and Preventing Illnesses and Injuries

Despite your best efforts to stay healthy and avoid illnesses and injuries, they are going to happen. Sometimes they will be mild and will not derail your training; other times they might require you to take time off from your training or even back out of a race. Generally, mild illnesses such as the common cold will not set you back in your training. While symptoms such as a runny nose and sore throat are uncomfortable, in most cases, they shouldn't stop you from running. If you have a cold and are still feeling strong enough to run, stick to your training schedule as planned. You might have to slow your pace slightly or cut back on your mileage, but as soon as the illness passes, you should be able to get right back on track with your training as planned. It might also be helpful to head to bed a bit earlier than usual until the cold passes, so your body gets the rest it needs to recover.

In the case of more severe illnesses, such as the flu, strep throat, bronchitis, or severe sinus infections, you might have to put your training on hold until your symptoms pass. Not only will running be nearly impossible when you are significantly ill; engaging in intense exercise could also prevent you from recovering quickly, resulting in you spending even more time sick in bed. Don't feel guilty about taking a few days or even a week off from training if it is necessary for your recovery. Take time to rest, see a doctor if needed, and pick up with your training when you regain your strength. If you have been diligent in adhering to your training plan, a week of missed training sessions shouldn't significantly impact your fitness levels.

While some illnesses are unavoidable, certain dietary supplements can promote immunity and prevent you from getting sick during bouts of intense training. Strasser et al. conducted a study with highly trained athletes during the winter months. One group of athletes in their study took probiotic supplements, whereas another group took a placebo pill. After twelve weeks, the athletes in the placebo group experienced an 11 percent decrease in levels of tryptophan, which is associated with immunity, whereas those in the probiotic group did not show any changes in tryptophan levels. Athletes who took the probiotic were also significantly less likely to suffer from symptoms of upper respiratory infections during the study period (759-760). Probiotics are not a panacea, but adding a supplement to your diet could reduce the number of colds you get during the winter months, so you can spend more time training and less time sick at home.

In addition to illnesses, injuries will sometimes require you to take time off from running in order to recover, but not all aches and pains become incapacitating injuries. When you are in the midst of your training, muscle soreness and stiffness are common and even expected, especially after longer runs or more intense training sessions, such as speed workouts. This soreness should improve with rest or an easy day, and as you adapt to the demands of training, you might find that you don't experience soreness as often.

On the other hand, if you have persistent aches and pains that make it difficult for you to complete workouts or maintain your usual running form, you might have a more serious injury. Common spots for such injuries include the feet, the knees, and the hips. If you have nagging pain, take some time off to rest for a few days, or engage in cross training workouts, such as swimming or riding an exercise bike. With any luck, the pain should subside, and you can return to training as usual. If the pain persists, it is probably necessary to consult with a sports medicine doctor who can help you to determine the cause of the injury and develop a treatment plan. The injury might require a few weeks of rest and or/cross training, as well as stretching exercises. If you are in the early or middle parts of your training and recover with at least a few weeks left before your race, you will likely be able to resume your training and compete in your race as scheduled, especially if you are running a shorter distance, such as the 5K or 10K. If you are running a full or half marathon, or if you have very little time left before your race, you might have to consider dropping out of the race and selecting another race to train for once you are healthy again. You can work with your doctor to come up with a plan of action and to determine when you are strong enough to resume training and competing.

While debilitating injuries happen to most runners at some point during their careers, there are steps you can take to protect yourself from a running-related injury. One such strategy is to avoid rapidly increasing your training volume. As discussed in several of the training plans in this book, when you are increasing your mileage to prepare for a race, it should be done slowly, perhaps adding one mile to your weekly long run every week or adding two to three miles to your total weekly mileage. You should also be cautious before jumping into a new training plan. For instance, if a sample training plan calls for you to start out running 30 miles per week during the first week and you have been averaging 20 miles per week, this sort of training plan is probably going to be too strenuous for you and could increase your risk of injury. If you find yourself in this sort of situation, you should first spend a few weeks building up your mileage until you are ready to tackle the higher-volume training plan, or consider using a less rigorous training plan. The research supports this approach. Nielsen et al. found that novice runners who increased their mileage by over 30 percent during a two-week period were at a higher risk of injury than runners who increased their running distance by under 10 percent were (739). Keep this in mind when using a training plan, and don't commit to any program that requires you to rapidly increase your mileage.

Similar to not increasing your running mileage too quickly, you should be cautious about running longer distance races, such as the marathon, if you are not prepared to do so. To protect yourself from injury, you should first gain experience with shorter distances before attempting a longer race. If you aspire to complete a full or half marathon, you might considering first training for and running 5K races, and then moving on to 10K races, and continuing to work your way up to the half or full marathon. The research supports gaining experience before running a longer race like the marathon. In a study of 943 marathon runners, van Poppel et al. found that those who had been running for fewer than five years were more likely to become injured (226). Interestingly, runners who didn't regularly complete interval training were also at an increased risk of injury, a finding which supports the inclusion of interval runs into your marathon training plan, as is recommended in the earlier chapter on preparing for a marathon.

The rest days that are incorporated into the sample training plans can also prevent you from developing a running-related injury. In a study of Finnish endurance athletes, including distance runners, Ristolainen et al. found that those who had few recovery days and the highest levels of training were at risk for overuse injuries (78). Your scheduled rest days can therefore play a critical role in keeping you strong and injury-free. Listen to your body; if you have an easy three-mile run scheduled but you are feeling especially sore and fatigued, you might benefit from taking the day completely off or engaging in some low-impact cross training, such as swimming, biking, or taking a leisurely walk. These easier days can be the difference between injury and health.

Based upon a review of the relevant research, it appears that slowly increasing your mileage and taking time to rest are useful approaches for injury prevention. You might be tempted to rapidly increase your mileage or jump into a marathon training program, but if you are too overzealous, you could end up with an incapacitating injury. Taking things slowly will pay off when you are able to remain strong and successfully make it to the finish line of your race. Allowing yourself time to recover and heal is important if you do develop an injury, and you might have to scale back your training to help your body recuperate from illnesses from time-to-time. If you take care of your body when it becomes ill or injured, you should recover quickly, and you will be able to meet your racing aspirations despite these minor setbacks. If, on the other hand, you continue to train intensely when your body is clearly in need of a break, you might end up on the sidelines for weeks, or even months.

Balancing Running with Other Commitments

Even if you manage to stay healthy and free from injuries, other obligations can sometimes get in the way of your training. Whether it's deadlines at work or your children's sports schedules, there are always going to be commitments that seem to take priority over running. Fortunately, it is possible to stick to your training despite a busy schedule. To adhere to your training amidst the chaos of life, pick a time of day when you know you will be able to commit to training. For some women, running first thing in the morning is the only option, so they set alarm clocks for 4:30 in the morning and get their workouts out of the way before other duties begin to call. Maybe this strategy will work for you, or perhaps you know there is no possibility that you're going to be able to drag yourself out of bed for a pre-dawn workout. If this is the case, select another time of day that works, whether it is in the evening after the kids go to bed, or during your lunch break. Whatever time you choose, what is most important is that it is a time during which you know you will consistently be able to commit to getting your training done. If you are having trouble choosing a time to complete your workouts, think about a time of day when you are least busy. Even the most hectic of schedules allow for some downtime. If you typically spend an hour in the evening browsing the Internet or catching up on your favorite shows, this might be the best time to schedule your workouts. Look for gaps or downtime in your routine, and make a plan to run during one of these periods.

Once you choose an ideal time for your workouts, it is also helpful to write down a schedule. If you're the computer savvy type, you can create a calendar or spreadsheet with your different workouts; if not, you might prefer to pencil in your workouts on a calendar or in a planner. Whichever method you prefer, having your workout schedule in front of you in writing will help you to stay committed. Treat your workouts just like you would a scheduled meeting or an appointment, and don't cancel them unless there are extenuating circumstances. Researchers have found that scheduling workouts in this manner is an effective method of remaining committed to a workout plan. A recent study involving middle-aged women found that including exercise in a daily routine was associated with adhering to physical activity, whereas disruptions in routine were barriers to exercise adherence (McArthur et al., 52).

Preparation is another factor that can enable adherence to an exercise program, such as training for a race. Being prepared involves planning and having your workout gear ready in advance (McArthur et al., 52). For a runner, preparation might mean sitting down every Friday evening and mapping out your running routes for the next week, or setting out your running shoes and outfit the night before a run so you are ready to go first thing in the morning. If you are prepared to run, it will be easier to stay committed to your daily workouts, because it won't take much time to get ready and out the door.

Preparation and a daily routine can help you stick to your training, but other obligations can still hinder your commitment to running. For women with children, family responsibilities can certainly impede their ability to adhere to a demanding training regimen. If you have children and feel that your training might limit your time with family, try to involve the kids in your running, and you might find that it is easier to stay committed. Take the family to the park on a Sunday afternoon, and you can run laps while the kids play on the jungle gym. You can also turn your races into a family outing. Let the kids have fun making signs prior to the race, and then they can participate as spectators and cheer you on from the sidelines. Some events also include one-mile fun runs for children, so your kids might even be able to join in on the fun of racing. Involving the kids turns your racing into an activity the whole family can enjoy, enabling you to stay committed to your training while also meeting the demands of motherhood.

Involving your family and utilizing other strategies for staying committed, such as planning ahead and creating a training schedule, can help you to balance time spent running with other obligations in your life. This doesn't mean it will always be easy to adhere to your training regimen, but by creating a plan that is consistent and suits your lifestyle, you will be more likely to stick to your training when life becomes hectic.

Maintaining Motivation

Having a routine can help you to stay committed to your running goals, but you might occasionally experience a lack of motivation, especially when your training becomes tough. After weeks or months of strenuous training, you will sometimes find that there are days that you feel tired, or you simply don't want to run. On these days, it can be easy to skip your workout or decide that you don't want to continue with your training. During the times you feel like throwing in the towel, it is important to restore your motivation. Fortunately, there are multitudes of different strategies that can motivate you to persevere with your training.

When you are feeling less than motivated, social involvement can help you to find a renewed sense of enthusiasm toward your training. For example, joining a running club that meets regularly to run together, or scheduling weekly long runs with a friend can increase your commitment to running. Accountability, in the form of others expecting you to participate in activities with them, has been documented in the research as empowering women to participate in exercise (McArthur et al., 53). If you know that a friend is counting on you to run with her on a Saturday morning, it will be harder to skip your workout. Simply telling friends and family members that you are preparing for a race could also motivate you to stick to your training, as you will feel accountable since others are aware of your plan to run a race (McArthur et al., 53). It will feel emotionally harder to back out of a race if your friends, coworkers, and spouse all expect you to run it.

Social involvement doesn't only hold you accountable to your running; it could also make the experience more enjoyable. In a study of college level distance runners, researchers found that running was more enjoyable for athletes when they ran with peers compared to when they ran alone (Carnes and Barkley, 257). It would be reasonable to conclude that you will be more motivated to run if you enjoy your workouts. You don't have to always run with a partner or a group to enjoy your training, but throwing in the occasional workout with a friend or joining in with the local running club a few times per month can help you to get through rough patches without throwing in the towel.

The act of setting goals for yourself can also motivate you to keep running. Wack et al. conducted a study with female runners in which participants set weekly goals, as well as a long-term goal, in addition to receiving performance feedback. Study results indicated that this method was effective, as all of the participants increased their running distance (181). You can maintain your motivation by setting a small goal to achieve every week, in addition to your long-term goal of completing a race within a certain time. Having a weekly goal allows you to celebrate small successes so you will be encouraged to keep training. Weekly goals can also seem less overwhelming than your long-term goal of competing in a race, and as you achieve your shorter term goals, your confidence in your running abilities should increase. If you are running a half marathon, for example, your long-term goal might be to complete the race in 1 hour and 45 minutes, whereas one of your weekly goals early in your training might be to complete a 10-mile run at a pace of 8:45 per mile. As your training progresses, you might aspire to run 45 miles in one week, or to complete a 15-mile run. You can also use this method for shorter races, such as the 5K. For week one, your goal might be to run 20 miles for the week, whereas for week four, you might aim to complete a five-mile run without stopping. You can use this goal-setting strategy as a motivation for races of any distance.

Running a race that supports a cause with which you identify can also serve to boost your motivation. Many races support some sort of charity, hospital, or local organization. For instance, large, popular races might benefit a children's hospital or a program within a health system. Smaller, local races might support a homeless shelter, community service agency, or a program within a school, such as the band or the track team. Select a race that supports a cause you stand behind, and the effort required for training will seem worthwhile to you. One participant in the study McArthur et al. conducted with middle-aged women shared this perspective, indicating that it was easier for her to exercise when she had a reason for it, and the researchers labeled this as "meaningful exercise" (52-53). Let a cause that you support be your reason for running, and you will be motivated to cross that finish line.

Running for charitable causes can encourage you to stay committed to training in general, but sometimes, showing dedication to specific types of workouts can be a struggle. If you find it challenging to make it through your long runs, something as simple as music can make it easier to endure them. Research has shown that when women listen to exciting music while performing aerobic exercise, they are able to work out for longer before becoming fatigued, and the exercise feels easier (RamezanPour, et al., 18).Create a playlist of your favorite melodies and tune in during long runs to make the time pass. Music is also an effective motivator during speed workouts. Lee and Kimmerly found that when runners listened to up tempo music while running on a treadmill, they ran faster than when they were listening to static noise, and they didn't report an increase in perceived exertion level (9-10). Listening to upbeat music can motivate you to pick up the pace and put forth your best effort during your training, and having an opportunity to listen to tunes you enjoy serves as a motivator to keep running.

When you are truly struggling with a lack of motivation, take the time to think about the reasons you run and the benefits that derive from your commitment to running. Write down the positives of running, and you will see that you have every reason to stay devoted to it. You can probably list a dozen benefits associated with running, including a feeling of accomplishment, improved self-esteem, better health, stress relief, weight control, and a sense of belonging with other runners. These sort of motivators are often the reason people keep running. In a study of marathon runners, Masters and Ogles found that veteran marathoners tended to cite their social identity as marathon runners as their main motivation to run, whereas novice runners were motivated by the health and weight management benefits, as well as the sense of goal attainment associated with marathon running. The researchers found that mid-level marathoners ran in order to reap psychological benefits and to improve their own performance (69). Tjelta et al. found similar results in a study of half marathon runners. Specifically, the women in their study reported competing in half marathons in order to exercise and challenge themselves. Women reported the following as their top three reasons for running in general: for physical and mental health benefits, for health issues, and because they found running to be fun (46-47).

Reasons to Keep Running

For Improved Health	To Develop a Sense of Accomplishment	For Weight Loss/Fat Loss	To Belong to a Community of Runers
To Set an Example for Children	To Relieve Stress	To Accomplish Personal Goals	To Socialize with Other Runners
To Enjoy Competition	To Support Charities	To Do Something Positive with Free Time	To Stay Physically Active

Whatever your motivation for running, it is clear that there are a plethora of reasons to keep hitting the pavement. Never forget the reasons you started running or the enjoyment you find in it. Even when training is tough, and life's obstacles stand in the way, it is important that women like you maintain a strong presence in the world of distance running. You owe it to the Roberta Gibbs, Katherine Switzers, and Joan Benoits of the world. These influential athletes were at the forefront of the women's running movement, and they made it clear that long distances were not reserved only for men. You, too, have the power to help this message live on for generations to come.

About the Expert

Jennifer Jacobsen is a wife and mother living in a small town in Northcentral Ohio, and she also happens to be a runner. She works fulltime for a public school but maintains a strong interest in running and physical fitness. She competes in local races throughout Ohio, and while she will run just about any distance, she specializes in the half marathon. Jennifer has won dozens of awards for being the top female finisher in local races, and she manages to keep up with her training while also balancing the demands of being a wife, mother, and professional. She has a passion for health and enjoys sharing her knowledge to help other women live up to their potential.

HowExpert publishes quick 'how to' guides on all topics from A to Z by everyday experts. Visit HowExpert.com to learn more.

Recommended Resources

- HowExpert.com – Quick 'How To' Guides on All Topics from A to Z by Everyday Experts.
- HowExpert.com/free – Free HowExpert Email Newsletter.
- HowExpert.com/books – HowExpert Books
- HowExpert.com/courses – HowExpert Courses
- HowExpert.com/membership – HowExpert Membership Site
- HowExpert.com/writers – Write About Your #1 Passion/Knowledge/Expertise & Become a HowExpert Author.
- HowExpert.com/resources – Additional HowExpert Recommended Resources
- YouTube.com/HowExpert – Subscribe to HowExpert YouTube.
- Instagram.com/HowExpert – Follow HowExpert on Instagram.
- Facebook.com/HowExpert – Follow HowExpert on Facebook.

Printed by BoD™in Norderstedt, Germany

9 781950 864874